D1716675

COLORFUL
MINDS

TIPS FOR
MANAGING
YOUR EMOTIONS

FUSION

The Pink Book

What to Do When You're Confused

by
John Wood

BEARPORT
PUBLISHING

Minneapolis, Minnesota

Credits

Cover and throughout – Ekaterina Kapranova, Beatriz Gascon J. 4-5– NLshop. 6–7 – faungfupix, KatyaNesterova, malerapaso/iStock. 10-11 – horina. illustrations, sherilhome, 123Done, ico, n0.com, Syuzann. 12-13 – GulArt, Padma Sanjaya, icon0.com, imaginima/iStock. 14-15 – Bibadash, Maica/iStock, Vitaly Zorkin/Shutterstock. 16-17 – emrcartoons.com, Kaidash, hudhud94, pepifoto/iStock. 18-19 – Gazoukoo, Mongta Studio/Shutterstock. 21 – MEDITERRANEAN/iStock.

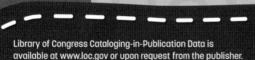

Library of Congress Cataloging-in-Publication Data is available at www.loc.gov or upon request from the publisher.

ISBN: 978-1-63691-872-3 (hardcover)
ISBN: 978-1-63691-880-8 (paperback)
ISBN: 978-1-63691-888-4 (ebook)

© 2023 Booklife Publishing

This edition is published by arrangement with Booklife Publishing.

For more information, write to Bearport Publishing, 5357 Penn Avenue South, Minneapolis, MN 55419. Printed in the United States of America.

For more The Pink Book activities:

1. Go to **www.factsurfer.com**

2. Enter **"Pink Book"** Into the search box.

3. Click on the cover of this book to see a list of activities.

CONTENTS

IMAGINE A RAINBOW

Red is angry.

Orange is for when I am **confident.**

Green is jealous.

Gold is when I feel proud.

The rainbow has a color for every feeling. Sometimes, one color shines brighter than the others.

4

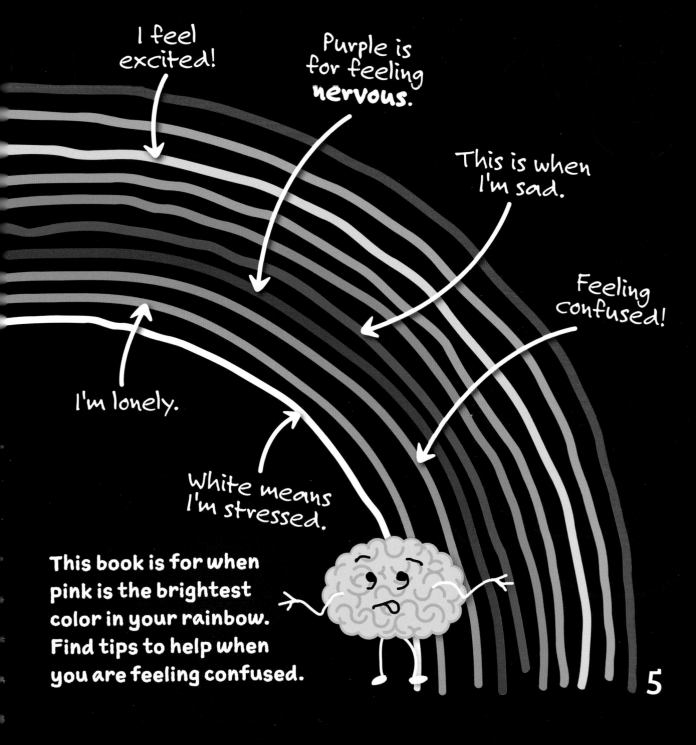

INVESTIGATE!

When we feel confused, we have trouble understanding something. Everybody gets confused sometimes, and it is nothing to be **embarrassed** about. Even the smartest adults get confused. Let's do an **investigation** to prove it.

HOW TO BE AN INVESTIGATOR

Make a list of three of the smartest adults you know. Ask them about times they have felt confused.

YOU COULD ASK QUESTIONS LIKE THESE!

Have you ever been confused about something?

Did you understand it later?

What did you do to help you understand?

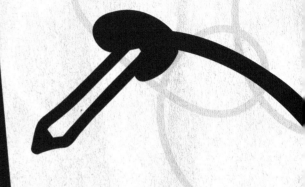

INVESTIGATION REPORT

Do smart people get confused? Yes!

7

FACTS TO
FOCUS ON

When we are confused, it can feel like our minds are spinning around and around. This is not a nice feeling at all. It makes everything very difficult to do.

If your mind feels like it is spinning, think about what you *do* know. It might help you calm your mind and stop it from spinning.

SAY THESE FACTS OUT LOUD!

My name is . . .

I am wearing . . .

The season is . . .

I am . . . years old.

Today is . . .

The weather outside is . . .

It is the month of . . .

TOP TIP!

You can repeat these simple facts any time you feel confused.

9

BRAIN WAYS

Sometimes things don't make sense when we learn them one way. But they become clear when we think another way.

There are lots of ways to learn things. We can read books, listen to someone explain something, or learn by doing it ourselves. Different people are better at learning in different ways.

CHOOSE ANY SUBJECT YOU WANT TO LEARN MORE ABOUT.

Now, look at the brain below and choose a way to learn about it. For example, you might learn about the weather where you live by watching a video.

Animals

Plants

Weather

Places

Learn by reading

Learn by listening

Learn by watching

Learn by making something or playing a game

TOP TIP!
Try different ways of learning until you find the right one for you.

11

A RELAXING ROOM

Have you ever been in a room that had a lot of colors, sounds, or things? How did it make you feel?

If you are already feeling confused, the room you are in could be making it worse.

Look at the things listed on the next page to see what might be adding to your feelings of confusion.

CONFUSION SPOTTER'S GUIDE

- Bright or colorful lights

- Flashing lights

- Shiny objects or things that are always moving

- Loud sounds

- High-pitched sounds

- Strong smells

- Smells you have not smelled before

Try to avoid these things to make your room more calming and **relaxing**.

DEAR DIARY

When we are confused, we might find it really hard to concentrate. A helpful way to **organize** our thoughts is to write them down.

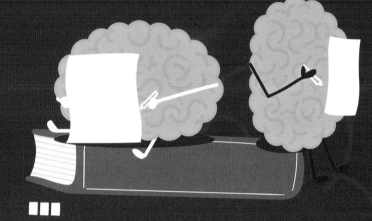

A diary is a blank book where we can write down things that are happening and how they make us feel.

Start your own diary. Look below to see what you might write about.

Tuesday, November 2nd

Dear Diary,

Today I felt confused about _____.
Being confused feels _____.

The part I found hardest was _____.
I think I can solve it by _____.

15

THE TIME MACHINE

It can be really hard to know what to do when we are confused. Slowing down can help us stay calm.

Use the time machine on the next page to take you forward to a time where you feel calmer.

To make the time machine work, slowly trace a circle around the clock. As you do this, breathe slowly and **deeply**. Imagine the clock's hands are moving, slower and slower until they stop.

TOP TIP!

Taking long, deep breaths and making slow circles with your finger can help you calm down in a hurry!

17

SUPER YOU

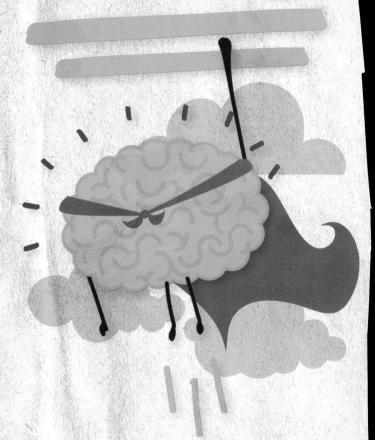

Sometimes we can't control our confusion. We might want to scream, run away, or cry. When we've calmed down, we might feel silly or embarrassed. That is okay!

When we feel like this, it is important to remember how super we are!

Grab a trusted adult or friend and follow the steps on the next page together.

STEP 1:

Grab some pencils and paper.

STEP 2:

Write something you are good at or why people like you. Don't let the other person see!

People like me because I can play the guitar.

STEP 3:

Now, ask the other person to do the same thing about you.

I like Anita because she plays cool songs.

STEP 4:

When you are both finished, show each other what makes you so super!

LITTLE IDEAS

There are many little tips and tricks we can use when we feel confused.

KEEP TALKING

Talking about our feelings can help us feel much better. Tell someone you trust why you feel confused.

QUESTION TIME

If you don't understand something, break it into little chunks. Then, ask for help with the part that confuses you.

WALK AWAY FROM YOUR PROBLEMS

Going outside and getting exercise can help you think more clearly and calmly.

LOOK AFTER YOURSELF

Eating healthy food and getting plenty of sleep may help you feel less confused.

TAKE A BREAK

If you are doing homework or **chores**, try to take a break and relax every hour or so.

zzzzzzzzz

FEELING BETTER?

Which tip worked best for you? Why do you think that is?

If you feel better, now is a good time to think about what made you feel confused and why. How might you handle things the next time you feel confused?

Every feeling you have is important! This book will still be here

whenever

you need it.

GLOSSARY

chores small jobs that are done regularly, often around the house

confident believing in one's abilities

embarrassed feeling confused, ashamed, or shy

investigation a way to find out the facts or the truth about something

nervous worried or afraid about what might happen

organize to arrange or plan things

relaxing resting to become calm

INDEX